# SHOW WINDOWS

Robert Benzio. B. Altman, New York, 1964. Lester Gaba said in *Women's Wear Daily*: "It's a bird's eye view, and window-shoppers get the feeling they're up on the ceiling peeping down on the players. The effect is accomplished by attaching the table and mannequins at right angles to the back wall, so that the tabletop and the gals' hats are parallel to the window glass."

# SHOW WINDOWS

## 75 YEARS OF THE ART OF DISPLAY

Barry James Wood

CONGDON & WEED, INC.

New York

Copyright © 1982 by Barry Wood
Library of Congress Cataloging in Publication Data
Wood, Barry, 1945-
Show windows.
1. Show-windows.   2. Clothing trade.
3. Jewelry trade.   I. Title.
HF5845.W68      659.1′57      81-12230
ISBN 0-86553-025-4
ISBN 0-312-92767-3 (St. Martin's)
Published by Congdon & Weed, Inc.
298 Fifth Avenue, New York, N.Y. 10001
Distributed by St. Martin's Press
175 Fifth Avenue, New York, N.Y. 10010
Published simultaneously in Canada by Thomas Nelson & Sons Limited
81 Curlew Drive, Don Mills, Ontario M3A 2R1
All Rights Reserved
Printed in the United States of America
Designed by Kathleen Westray
First Edition

TO LEE FORREST NYDEGGER,
who says he owes it all to
Jeanette MacDonald and Charles Laemmle

# PREFACE

THE IDEA FOR THIS BOOK CAME TO ME ONE morning about three years ago, as the result of a conversation with a friend, Lee Nydegger, about a world he knew well—the world of store windows. Lee, a display artist, spent several hours describing his experiences behind the glass, telling me his thoughts on window display as an art. He had opened the door on a beguiling and little-known world, and my curiosity was enlivened.

I started to look more closely at the store windows I passed during my daily travels around New York City. When I came upon a display that captured my attention, I would try to analyze what it was that moved me and why. I went to the library to dig up more information, but discovered a dearth of material on the subject: Most of the articles had been written twenty or thirty years ago, and the only three significant books I unearthed had been published in the early fifties.

The major source of information was the trade's principal journal, *Display World* (now entitled *Visual Merchandising*). It appeared that historians had not taken this area of endeavor very seriously and that display as an art form had been largely ignored.

One article, however, had appeared in *Art News*. It gave a vivid description of people lured to windows in the financial district of New York in the thirties: "One has only to note the crowds that gather around any window display of striking originality to realize how eagerly the populace responds to any change in the standardized fare which is fed it. Windows . . . in this period of depression . . . do little, save whet the appetite for the unattainable. And yet there are few people without an inner kernel of wonder and imagination that may be touched and stimulated." This statement came closest to echoing my own feelings. And, as I worked on this book, I discovered there were others who shared my feelings—a large group of window aficionados who had seldom spoken of their affair.

It was then that I began to search for evidence of windows that, as Annie Beaumel of Hermès had once put it, were "not just an array of goods but works of imagination, of caprice, of fantasy, of color." It was soon apparent, however, that the work of the window display artist was rarely considered very important by the stores, given the generally cavalier treatment of photographic records of the windows.

Though no display lasted more than a couple of weeks, and a photograph was the only means of recording its brief existence, many stores had thrown out their collections, not wishing to pay storage costs or to be encumbered by the bulk.

Others had negligently piled photographs in boxes and bins stashed in the cobwebbed corners of basements. I regularly found myself covered with dirt, sifting through a farrago of forgotten and often faded photographs, some as fragile as gold leaf. I felt like an archeologist on an expedition when I did manage to locate, among the strata of yellowed clippings, a few visual gems from a world that no longer existed. Occasionally, some unknown secretary had dutifully filed photographs in albums, but often the glue had seeped beyond the edges and the pages had stuck together. In separating them, I found it impossible not to damage the reproductions. Only at Lord & Taylor had any concentrated effort been made to organize and protect the pictures.

As part of my quest, I sought out the men and women who were, or are, involved in the fishbowl profession of window display. To locate them in their natural habitat, I often had to travel through the bowels of buildings, traverse storage, furnace, and air-conditioning rooms, or go up and down fire stairs. The location of many a display director's office soon made clear to me the ambiguous position that he or she held in the store hierarchy. Once discovered, these people were willing—even eager—to talk of their experiences and feelings about their glassed-in world.

From what I learned, it seems evident that display artists are destined forever to be people in the middle—suspended, as one display artist put it, "between business and art, between the direct and practical object of selling and the aspiration of the artist."

Although many store managers acknowledge the importance of the display artist's role in the functioning of the store, they are also fearful of the waves that may be stirred by an unusual or unconventional window, and often use every chance they get to clip the wings of the display artist. There are exceptions, of course. Some leading display artists are recognized as vital ingredients in a store's success and are officed and treated accordingly. But many more complain that the store managers still consider them just another part of the maintenance crew along with the porters, janitors, and stock clerks.

Often, this ambiguity of role continues outside the store. Unlike painters or dancers, display people have no identifiable professional image. There is no coterie, official or unofficial, to give them a feeling of community. "Market week," the twice-yearly gathering at which new display products are exhibited, is usually the only time display people get together. Otherwise, they are seldom, if ever, in contact with one another.

According to one unknown source, the display artist is constantly expected to "square the circle by designing windows that are 'straight' yet somehow special, hackneyed yet new, striking yet not upsetting, surprising yet all the time conventional." In practice, it is the work of inspired but less tractable individuals, those who have refused to subordinate beauty to politics and pure merchandising, that has won me over. In the final analysis, the amount of money, time, and energy spent creating a window, the quantity of detail, props, or sets incorporated in it, are no measure of its effectiveness.

Lyricism of design, vivacity of concept, drama—these are the criteria Lee Nydegger and I used to select the photographs in this book. We eschewed windows based on the use of props, because props are so often a dull, safe substitute for imagination and daring. We tried to choose windows that not only illustrate the ephemerality of the art but also reveal its many facets, such as the delicate skill of draping—spilling curtains, dresses, bolts of cloth into exquisite patterns whose flow and precise folds would be impossible to reproduce today even if the same materials were available.

There are more photographs in this book from New York than from other cities. This does not mean that creative work is not done elsewhere; it is just that New York has always been the acknowledged capital of display, the place where rebellious and innovative ideas have had the best chance of succeeding. New York is also the last major city to give prominence to windows; in many other cities, more energy is devoted to store interiors.

I have made an effort to credit the actual designers of the windows rather than the directors of display departments, when such information was available. It should be remembered, however, that display is essentially a collaborative undertaking and that the people who do hair, makeup, dressing, positioning, and lighting also deserve recognition. While it is impossible to mention them all, they know who they are.

These display artists have provided the world with an art that is as much a counterpoint to the reality of everyday life as the purple petals of the bold crocus are to the bleakness of a seemingly endless winter. We search endlessly for that which can temporarily lift us out of the tedious routine and narrow self-involvement of our everyday lives and magically transport us to another world where our senses are stirred and our imaginations refreshed. To those who are sensitive to beauty and still capable of wonder, the display artists can offer just such a trip. Because of the hope their spirit symbolizes, I have written this book.

# CONTENTS

PREFACE    vii

BEHIND THE WINDOW GLASS    3

A BRIEF HISTORY    13

THE PHOTOGRAPHS    19

TOM LEE    129

DANA O'CLARE    135

HENRY CALLAHAN    143

ROBERT BENZIO    149

CANDY PRATTS    153

GENE MOORE    161

If, of thy mortal goods thou art bereft
And from thy slender store two loaves alone
To thee are left,
Sell one, and with the dole
Buy hyacinths to feed the soul.

SAADI *(13th century)*

# SHOW WINDOWS

# BEHIND
# THE WINDOW GLASS

EVERY DAY, MILLIONS OF PEOPLE STREAM BY the windows of department stores, turning their heads as they pass, perhaps stopping to peer in at something behind the glass. But few of them realize that those exhibits are the work of an unusual group of people who have toiled behind papered windows to produce the lovely, but transitory, effects. The exciting visions of these men and women—the display artists—create a vast and enthralling museum of window display, a museum whose exhibits are in constant flux.

By its very nature, display is synonymous with change. Two weeks, at the most, is the allotted lifetime for most window displays—a short span for a work of art. But it is art nonetheless. Display artists are creators, seers who capture and distill images in which we look at ourselves and our fantasies.

Windows are theater. When we gaze into a store window, we become part of a ticketless audience of far vaster numbers than any Broadway house has ever seated. We witness a drama, frozen behind the glass, that reflects the display artist's humor or solemnity, his awareness or his prejudices, his despair or his dreams. If he communicates his theme in a provocative and convincing way, he has the power to bring those dreams to life, to cast a spell, and to capture that which is most elusive of all—our imaginations.

"We are the butterflies of the art world," says one eminent display artist. Restlessly drifting in and out of the window world, the display artist pollinates his field from a lush and varied bouquet drawn from theater, dance, photography, design, and painting. Because of the constant demand to produce new environments, to move beyond the last statement, he feasts upon the *au courant*—any new image or idea that appears in film, journals, books, current events, fashion shows, or that comes up in conversation may fuel his creativity. A display artist's antennae are always tuned to the new. As a result, display artists are true reflections of their time, their compositions often the first tangible expression of a current that may later turn into a tidal wave.

Display art also experiments with the latest products of science—spun glass, dry ice, plastics, stainless steel, fluorescent lighting, neon, acrylics, chrome, laser light—materials chosen for their artistic and suggestive qualities rather than for their utilitarian functions. Display artists often act as trail guides in their bold exploration of the unknown.

To pin down this elusive butterfly, to analyze the qualities that make up a successful display artist, is close to impossible. Every display person is eventually asked, "Did you go to school for that or did you get it out of your head?" For most of them, the answer is the latter. Display is an art that requires mastery of a multitude of skills, the teaching of which runs counter to the specialized training found in conventional art schools. Those who work in the field have usually learned their techniques through an apprenticeship. But even the expert knowledge of theory, design, lighting, color, and material necessary to conceive a meticulous draft is no guarantee of the creation of striking or memorable window art. More frequently, it takes a mixture of rare and intangible qualities: inspiration, inventiveness, spontaneity, and—most important of all—daring and innovation that constantly challenge the boundaries of convention.

One story tells of a display artist who was in a window installing a large pier glass, when he accidentally struck and broke it. Rather than despair, he put his hammer into the mannequin's hand and placed her next to the shattered mirror. Another tells of a man who was able to drape polyester on a mannequin so that it looked like a $10,000 Saint Laurent gown. As display artist Jim Buckley says, "Improvisation is the core of display's vitality."

Butterflies they may be, but behind the windows, these butterflies labor like bees. For window art is not only flair, magic, and beauty; it is also the decidedly less appealing behind-the-scenes drudgery. To create and execute a window, a display artist must be carpenter, metal worker, plasterer, painter, paperhanger. He or she must understand the structural qualities of a myriad of display materials and be familiar with the various tools and techniques used with them. Knowledge of mechanical engineering and electrical work is usually necessary because most department store windows were designed by architects unaware of the requirements of window display. Walls that will not take a staple, limited lighting outlets and placements, ceilings that were never designed to support a 500-pound chandelier, lack of refrigeration ruling out the use of perishables—all these problems demand ingenuity and adaptation.

Because windows lack depth and expanse, display artists, as designers of interior space, must also have a sense of spatial relationships. It is quite a challenge to overcome architectural limitations and to make the most creative use of such a restricted "canvas." Display artists must always stay abreast of the latest trends and styles, search out new decorative sources, become familiar with fixture and carpeting methods, and learn color and lighting relationships.

Effective lighting is a key factor in the staging of a successful window. A display artist faces unusual problems as he tries to build a theatrical atmosphere. Weather, for example, is a major concern. The designer must take into account everything from blazing sun to pitch of night. He must gear his window for daylight effectiveness to capture the shoppers' attention, yet he also wants a window that will glow against the enveloping black. He must eliminate reflection and glare so that light does not compete with the object displayed and detract from its dramatic quality. The job is made more difficult when, as is often the case, windows do not have sufficient current or outlets. Special equipment has been developed to overcome these limitations. And some stores employ expert electricians to operate central light switchboards, thus ensuring that a window is romantically dim rather than gloomy or garish. When done well, lighting heightens impact and creates drama; it can make a mediocre display unforgettable.

Display artists must also handle mannequins—not generally known for their expert design or easy responsiveness. Great patience and dexterity are required to turn these lifeless, rigid bodies into expressive, animated creatures simply by manipulating their attitudes and postures.

The clothing itself may be a problem. A display artist must constantly contend with clothes he would never have chosen to present in the window—clothes too bland, or too fussy—some even ridiculous. Veils may have to be chopped, bows added, feathers removed, dresses put on the mannequin backwards to make it exciting—work that may keep him in the window until dawn.

During the course of a year, hundreds of props are received and returned, and it is the display artist's responsibility to be certain they are not lost or misplaced. The same applies to merchandise: If it does not get back to the department it came from, the cost is deducted from the display budget.

Most display artists agree on one point: There is virtually no job in the store so demeaning that they haven't had to do it at one time or another. The nature of the art takes a display person from the store's basement to its attic, often carting his equipment along with him. At one time, a well-known New York store expected its display artists to help unload trucks. There is no doubt that physical strength is an asset in this often arduous job.

"Display is not glamorous," says one display artist. "The end product may be, but certainly not the road to it." Even cleaning up the display department, or washing the huge windows, often falls to the late-night staff of display artists who are toiling to present a clean, fingerprint-free vista to the public the next day. A store window is not like the theater, where a raised stage or the distance of an orchestra pit separates viewers from the scene before them. The public is not only eye level with the display but also up close to it. Every mote of dust, each withered flower, any minute flaw is readily apparent to the audience of pedestrians.

The greatest difficulty of the vocation of display, however, is to walk the delicate line that separates art from merchandising. In larger stores, it is the display director who maintains the balance between business and art. It is up to him to keep the representatives of these two groups not only on speaking terms but working together productively.

Most display directors have previously been window artists. Once they take over the director's job, they are seldom able to participate firsthand in either the conception or the execution of the windows. That work is delegated to assistants, or apprentices, who understand the overall image the director wants to achieve. The director's job is then to edit the results. To get the best results, he must support and encourage his team of artists, cultivating the boldness, spontaneity, and infectious enjoyment that it takes to create striking windows. Remembering the importance of "camping" in the window, he must not give in to management's conformist priorities at the expense of his people's morale. If he does, the store will suffer, because the windows will be dreary rather than inspired.

But the display director must also maintain the good will of the store management, which provides him his budget. In fact, the business of money—getting it, appropriating its use, accounting for its expenditure—is a large part of the job. The display director decides how much to invest in properties, when to spend, and when to save.

The display director's position requires insight and diplomacy. Coordinating the wishes and needs of a vast army of people—the carefully selected display team, the janitors and stock clerks who help out, the buyers and fashion personnel, the store executives—is a delicate job. Much time is spent smoothing ruffled feathers, pacifying prima donnas, defusing jealousies and rivalries, and catering to a variety of firm likes and dislikes. One president of B. Altman, for instance, prohibited the use of peacock feathers, violets, and the color purple in the windows because to him the color evoked funerals. Even a cluster of grapes was once removed from a display at his command. Designers and buyers are also famous for interfering with windows if they don't approve of the concept, the props, or the accessories. One well-known couturier actually set fire to one of her own gowns because two mannequins portrayed as guests at a party were wearing the identical costume.

Another problem is that management, still adjusting to last year's styles, may be horrified by up-to-date displays. Marketing directors and department heads also scrutinize the windows, and have even been known to come in and take an item so they can sell it. The short life of the window is thus made even shorter.

Many window artists find it difficult to accept the short life of their work, to watch as it is demolished week after week. In a year, they may have to create as many as two thousand windows, each of which should be fresh and original. The sense of loss can be demoralizing. It is increased if the store will not pay to photograph these ephemeral works of art. Many display artists eventually leave the field to avoid the frustration; others gradually slip into unhappy routine, installing only perfunctory displays.

Display artists agree that they are often hampered professionally and creatively. Says one of them, "The more commonplace the window, the more acceptable it is; the more beautiful and provocative, the more controversial." Painters, sculptors, and other artists are generally given unlimited freedom to be controversial. Not so the display artist. Store management is wary, fearful for propriety and for the store's reputation. The very boldness and creativity that enable a display person to forge exciting new images week after week may prove disconcerting or even threatening to management. A few superstar display artists are handled with kid gloves, but most of them are carefully supervised. It is an uncomfortable position. Another person noted, "The artistic nature cannot survive in a soulless shop win-

11

dow dedicated to increasing sales." And, furthermore, display people feel that store managers should realize that truly imaginative windows are the best public relations tool a store can have.

One enterprising Cartier president (1967–1969), Joseph Liebman, decided to determine to what degree unfettered creative windows would increase sales. As an experiment, he gave complete artistic freedom to his display person, Ray Mastrobuoni, to concentrate solely on the appearance of the window and not on the selling of merchandise. All the clerks then asked the customers who looked at merchandise to give their reasons for coming into the store. The percentage of customers who entered the store as a direct result of the windows was so high that Liebman gave the display department an unlimited budget and continued freedom to create whatever it wished. The lesson: Beauty entices and attracts. No selling operation can afford to ignore the fact that striking windows can be used to create and reinforce a store's image, not just to sell goods.

Geraldine Stutz, the president of Henri Bendel, is one executive who has agreed with the display artists. "Windows are not meant to sell merchandise or even to show it," she told *Women's Wear Daily* in 1968. "They are two eyes to communicate the spirit and point of the store."

# A BRIEF HISTORY

FROM THE BEGINNING, WINDOW DISPLAYS have mirrored the society around them, reflecting but also shaping the tastes and fantasies of their time. Lined up one after the other, they would form a stunning series of tableaux embodying the history of our ideas, our emotions, our unconscious longings. Windows are always immediate, always accessible, always up-to-date—and they may well be America's most popular art form.

At the end of the nineteenth century, store windows as we now know them—windows that displayed merchandise to the passing public—were born. The earliest ones evoked the gilded age of Victorian opulence—and the Victorian propriety that was in the air. Often, they were elaborate theatrical exhibitions that drew upon Egyptian, Persian, Greek, and Roman art and architecture for inspiration: Temples, columns, urns, garlands, vines, swags of silk flowers, topiary, and stuffed peacocks were favorite props of window trimmers of the time. The windows were invariably lined with walnut, mahogany, caen-stone, or travertine—unyielding surfaces that were not often adaptable to the trimmer's imagination and could only be used for the hanging of draperies, fabric, or paintings.

The early windows were populated by dressmaker's forms or, if the store could afford them, 200-pound wax mannequins, usually imported from France and Germany, but sometimes made locally. These mannequins, first introduced at the Paris Exposition of 1894, mirrored the prevailing concept of beauty. They were startlingly realistic, with genuine hair and eyelashes, glass eyes, and false teeth.

Unfortunately, the wax mannequins did not stand up to the elements. They melted in the intense heat generated in the window during the summer and cracked during winter's icy embrace. Display people carried candles to mend the fallen fingers and drooping ears, wearing hats so that they would not be mistaken for janitors.

Occasionally, cast-iron mannequins, even heavier at 300 pounds each, were used, most often to show men's clothes, but the Herculean effort required to move them made them extremely unpopular. In most cases, both wax and iron "dummies," as they were called, were supported by a heavy metal base with one prong running up the foot, necessitating a hole in both shoe and stocking.

The Women's Christian Temperance Union of New York City, in

true Victorian style, issued protests against the use of the realistic wax figures, but were especially upset that the display artists dressed them in full view of the public. The mannequins were not abandoned, but to pacify the WCTU, window trimmers started to paper the windows while they worked. As it turned out, the papering may have been an unexpected gain—even today it is used to keep the window a secret and to build up suspense until the artist is ready to reveal his creation.

Gas, kerosene, or gasoline was still being used in the lamps that lit many stores at the turn of the century, but gradually some of the more progressive emporiums started to change over to electric light. Naked bulbs were used and were focused by means of metal reflectors; softer light was produced by coating the bulbs first with glue, then with talcum powder or sugar. Shellac mixed with a dye and painted on the bulb provided colored light.

Before 1925, a "let's show 'em everything we got" syndrome prevailed, and windows were flooded with hundreds or thousands of pieces of merchandise arranged in intricate designs or geometric structures—pyramids of spools, pencils, and harmonicas; fans of nails, scissors, and thimbles; ships of handkerchiefs, bibs, and socks—all arrayed with painstaking attention to detail.

The first significant change in windows occurred toward the end of the 1920s when budget cutbacks seriously curtailed the previously ornate style: Simpler, cleaner display was born. Design attitudes had also been influenced by the 1925 Paris Exposition Internationale des Arts Décoratifs. Mannequins became less realistic, more stylized. The sober background of dark wood or cold stone gradually disappeared, as did artificial foliage and flowers. Lighting took on a subtler, more sophisticated look; now it was used not only for illumination but to create a dramatic mood. At B. Altman, for example, white panels, aluminum tubes, and lambent opal glass replaced the harsh look of mahogany under bare light bulbs.

In the thirties, Surrealism took the window world by storm. Trompe l'oeil sets gave the windows a new magic and provided a fresh illusion of space. Sleek, abstract mannequins—often headless or limbless—stopped passers-by in their tracks. Mannequins were now made of plaster or papier-mâché, and novel materials like plastic and seamless paper began to revolutionize the field.

Store windows had never been more chic. During the Depression, display artists strove to present a reassuring image of well-being and prosperity to help the public forget the gloomy economic reality. Another exposition in Paris in 1937, and two in New York in 1939 and 1940, also provided a welcome infusion of energy and imagination to the field. Many studios were set up to produce sets exclusively for windows. The golden age of window display had begun.

World War II, however, took its toll on window design. Since fewer materials and resources were available, dressing a window demanded the utmost in ingenuity. But the show went on, often availed of large budgets that reflected not only the increased competition among merchandisers to sell a limited amount of goods, but also the official recognition that windows could provide a psychological means of whipping up patriotism. Most stores had at least one display devoted to the war cause, urging window shoppers to get behind the fighting men, to be thrifty, and to buy war bonds.

Immediately after World War II window budgets grew prodigiously. Manufacturers had to reestablish their relationship with the new buying public that was rapidly attaining affluence, and display was acknowledged as a powerful means of wooing customers into the stores. Windows became "stagy"; props proliferated. Mannequins made of fiberglass, paper, plastic, and wire were introduced, but most of them were still stiff, awkward to use, and difficult to pose in natural positions. In the sentimental atmosphere of the late forties and fifties, windows were often decorated with huge cut-out hearts and lots of lace. Window artists today still refer to those as the days of "paper hearts." The era also favored big, prop-oriented windows in which the mannequins would invariably stand with arms akimbo. Plastic plants and flowers of greater realism began to appear. Double-faced tape was invented, which allowed designers to give garments a windblown look, relieving the static window tableaux. But even with these technical advances, the store windows of the fifties reflected the general blandness of the decade: They were safe, predictable, and, with a few notable exceptions, dull.

In the sixties, more realistic and flexible mannequins from England and Europe were introduced. These mannequins were wired, so there was no need for the unsightly base and pole. Even ethnic mannequins were created. Once again display took off into the unknown.

By the seventies, valences, ceilings, and dividers were being ripped out to create banks of windows. Props were used less—the windows were either filled with mannequins or left almost empty, just one lone figure cowering in a corner against a structural column. If the windows of the sixties glittered with mirroring, mylar, glass, and silver balls, then the seventies windows were pearlized with brushed aluminum, bronze, and gold that recalled the swank thirties. And lest the business take itself too seriously, kinky-chic psychodrama windows provided provocative relief.

Ephemerality is the very essence of window art. Every one of these windows, every artifact of the evolution of window display, has disappeared. It may be that with corporate control and the trend toward formula windows, creativity itself will disappear. If so, this book will be a eulogy for the bold individuals who have given us the ephemeral art of display.

# THE PHOTOGRAPHS

Designer unknown. T. Eaton Company, Toronto, 1908. One of the earliest surviving photographs of window display—an extravaganza of furs.

22 | Designer unknown. T. Eaton Company, Toronto. A window done in 1918 to celebrate the end of World War I.

Designer unknown. Lord &
Taylor, New York, early 1920s.
Wax mannequins were prone
to melt under hot lights. In this
case, the "illuminator" was
shielded by a Boston fern.

23

J. R. PALMENBERG'S SONS, Inc.

New York          Chicago

Boston          Baltimore

San Francisco

Head No. 3

Left Arm No. 3          Right Arm No. 4

24

J. R. PALMENBERG'S SONS, Inc.
New York          Chicago
Boston            Baltimore
San Francisco

Head No. 6
Left Arm No. 2          Right Arm No. 3

Designer unknown. Early 1920s. Salesmen's photographs from J. R. Palmenberg Sons, Inc., a manufacturer of wax mannequins. Stores ordered from catalogues of these photos, which afforded them the opportunity to choose a combination of heads and arms to go with basic torsos.

25

26 | Designer unknown. Lord & Taylor, New York, early 1920s. Headless iron mannequins displayed boys' clothes—Norfolk jackets and knickers—while model airplanes whirred above them (the blurred images above the lamps).

Designer and store unknown. Springfield, Mass., about 1925. The window artists' trade journal, *Display World*, called this period the time of "'torturing' the merchandise, when the displayman who could get the most articles in a given space was rated higher than one who could not."

27

28 | Designer unknown. B. Altman, New York, about 1925. A sea of rumpled satin, inspired by the satin rosette detailing on the costume.

Designer and store unknown. Mid-1920s. Some window artists are expert with fabric, able to drape it naturally from the bolt. In this case, the dress was created right on the mannequin, *in situ*, just by folding and pinning.

29

30 | Designer unknown. White's, Boston, 1924. Wax mannequins, often imported from Europe, were now becoming increasingly realistic.

Designer unknown. T. Eaton Company, Toronto, 1924. By the sea, complete with sand. One of the earliest examples of bringing the outdoors in.

31

Designer and store unknown.
1924. A wax bride.

32

Designer unknown. Probably Marshall Field's, Chicago, about 1925. Wisteria ran rampant in this tableau of spring fashions. On the back of the original photograph are the measurements "Bust-33, Hip-35"—then the dimensions of ideal female beauty.

33

34 | Designer unknown. B. Altman, New York, about 1925. Ornate lampshade, ornate dresses.

Designer unknown. T. Eaton Company, Montreal, about 1925. An array of "Chapeaux de Paille."
Eaton was one of the few retailers to make an archive of display photographs.

35

36

Designers unknown. Two displays from Dickson–Ives of Orlando, Florida, and (*overleaf*) two from Yowell, Drew, & Ivey, the store across the street, 1925 and 1926. Competition between stores often produced departures—such as these skillful creations of everyday scenes.

37

38

39

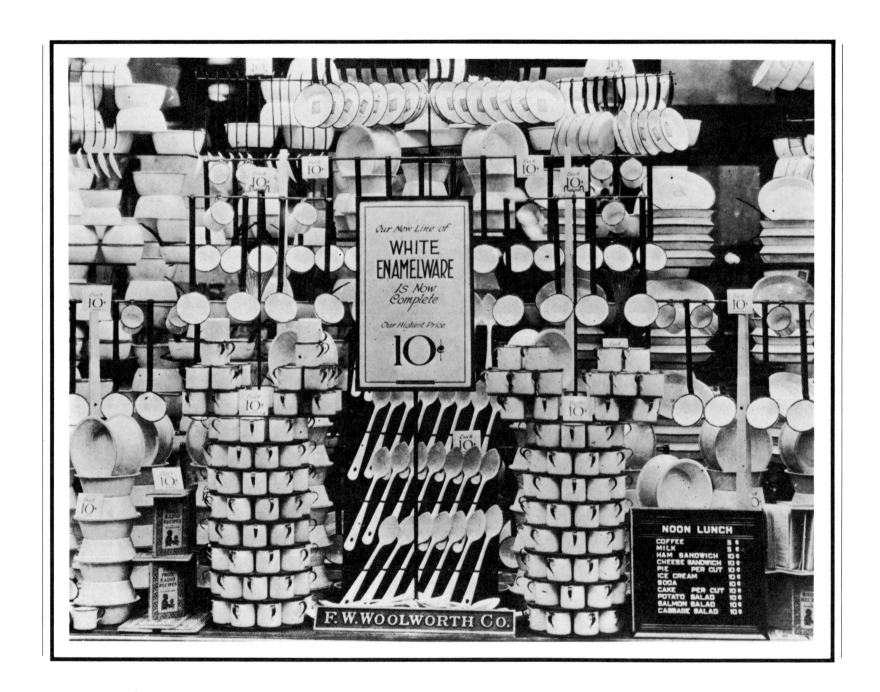

Designers unknown. Woolworth's (*left*) and T. Eaton Company, Toronto (*above*), mid-1920s. Hundreds of tin cups, and a cascade of dolls for Christmas: two displays faithful to the principle that more is more.

42

Jules J. Brodeur. Richard Hudnut, New York, 1925, 1927, and 1928. Brodeur was one of the earliest display artists to distinguish himself. He was the first to use small, shadowbox windows scaled down to the size of the merchandise—in this case, cosmetics. He was well known for his extravagant use of miniature flowers, stiffened velvet bows (although the one on the dressing table here is gold lamé), feathers, sequins, and jewels. Concentrated opulence became his trademark. Acknowledged for his skill at draping, he was said to have the flair of a couturier. He was display director at Coty from 1941 until his death; all records of his work there were thrown out when the firm emptied its storage rooms several years ago. These photographs, signed by Brodeur, were found in the New York Public Library.

43

44

Designer unknown. Late 1920s. The flapper era, here represented by two stylized mannequins with molded, air-brushed hair, from Leopold C. Schmidt, "sculptor and manufacturer."

45

46 | Designer unknown. Filene's, Boston, 1927. A woman trying to choose between her wigs. The wigs on wax mannequins were always made of real hair, as were the wigs for humans.

Dick Wallace. B. Altman, New York, about 1930. By the thirties, ornate windows were a thing of the past. At B. Altman, the mahogany was covered over by white panels, and bare bulbs gave way to light diffused though opal glass. Lester Gaba made the mannequin on the left, which was modeled after Mrs. Harrison Williams, a society woman of the day.

47

48 | Henry Callahan. Bonwit Teller, Philadelphia, 1933. Callahan celebrated "Fashion's Declaration of Independence" with abstract fireworks.

Lester Gaba. Best & Co., New York, 1934. Gaba designed not only the display, but also the mannequins, which were known as the Gaba Girls. Inspired by the zebra rug, he designed the striped cape and did the zebra painting. He also sculpted miniature mannequins from soap for the small display box at the far left.

50 | Sidney Ring. Saks Fifth Avenue, New York, 1932. Ring was known for three "signature objects"—
a chiffon handkerchief, a rope of pearls, and a perfume bottle—two of which are incorporated
into this design.

Sidney Ring. Saks Fifth Avenue, New York, 1937. Cool, crisp, and clean was Saks's new image for
the thirties. Under Surrealist influence, Ring allowed sporting clothes to float against a ribbed
background, attached by only one abstract arm to chair or column.

52 | Tom Lee. Bonwit Teller, New York, 1937. A window festooned with tulle made a tent for a "Mystic Maharani" posed pensively on the sands of time.

Tom Lee. Bonwit Teller, New York, 1937. Lee posed this elegant abstract mannequin in a setting whose simplicity is relieved only by a wisp of tulle. The show card, under the heading "Form Divine," declares, "The new clothes ask you to be proudly erect, with bosom lifted, waistline tiny."

54 | Tom Lee. Bonwit Teller, New York, 1937. A black nude mannequin was veiled in black *point d'esprit* to show off "Well's Perfume Noir for Sophisticates in Black." Perfume windows were usually allowed somewhat more license than those showing other products.

Tom Lee. Bonwit Teller, New
York, 1939. "Airspun Hosiery."
Angel's hair, or spun glass,
painful to use but able to give a
cloudy, ethereal effect, was
shown in windows long before
it was used on Christmas trees.
Materials newly developed by
science were often seized upon
by display people and put to
uses not conceived of in the
laboratory.

55

Tom Lee. Bonwit Teller, New York, 1938. The wig and eyelashes were made by Lee, who was skilled as a paper sculptor.

56

Tom Lee. Bonwit Teller, New York, 1939. The photographic portrait was specially commissioned to tie in with this window's tropical theme.

57

58 | Tom Lee. Bonwit Teller, New York, 1940. A fanciful mermaid emerged from an ocean of tulle and foam of feathers, proclaiming the birth of a new perfume—Tailspin.

Tom Lee. Bonwit Teller, New York, 1940. Carmen Miranda starred in this "Brazilian Bravura" display at the same time that she starred in the Broadway musical *Sons o' Fun*.

59

Tom Lee. Bonwit Teller, New York, 1940. Enveloped in sealskin and surveying the public with glacial hauteur, this mannequin was fashioned after top *Vogue* model Helen Bennet.

60

Tom Lee. Bonwit Teller, New York, 1940. The sumptuous train of this silk jersey wedding gown was painstakingly arranged in intricate folds.

62 | Dana O'Clare. Lord & Taylor, New York, 1940. Swaths of material were draped to emphasize the construction of the turbans.

Dana O'Clare. Lord & Taylor, New York, 1940. A boudoir of meretricious luxury floated in the night sky, with putti attending.

64 | Dana O'Clare. Lord & Taylor, New York, 1941. Society ladies preparing for the Allied Relief Ball— a harbinger of war.

Gene Moore. Bonwit Teller,
New York, 1945. As the show
card says, a theatrical
"Champagne Fantasy."

65

66

Arthur Long and Gene Moore. Bonwit Teller, New York, about 1945. The clothes as well as the display were inspired by a Vermeer exhibit going on at the time. During the war, store windows were equipped with blackout curtains to foil enemy bombers.

Designers unknown. B. Altman, New York, 1944 (*above*); Lord & Taylor, New York, somewhat later (*right*). During World War II all the major department stores devoted at least one window to patriotic propaganda. This one urged the purchase of war bonds with a fervor previously re-

served for dry goods. A later, grimmer window showing a bombed-out bedroom brought the war close to home.

70 | Gene Moore. Bonwit Teller, New York, 1949. Moore says, "I wanted to show a woman who loved hats so much she grew an extra head to wear them."

Gene Moore. Bonwit Teller, New York, 1949. "Wanted: Night White" was one of a series of tableaux. "The girl in the mask was holding up the other to get what she was wearing," Moore explains.

72

Tommy Rowland. W & J Sloane, New York, 1949. Rowland is one of the few female window artists. Here she created a New York patrician Christmas that has long since disappeared.

74 | Bob Foster. B. Altman, New York, 1950. Stripes, plaid, and floral print chiffon are contrasted in an artfully abundant arrangement.

Henry Callahan. Lord & Taylor, New York, 1950. This handkerchief angel was a masterpiece of pinning, created to display a maximum number of samples while retaining a theme.

Jim Buckley. Saks Fifth Avenue, Beverly Hills, early 1950s. "Papa, Won't You Dance with Me?" Wax mannequins had all but disappeared by the time these two were used—to promote women's shoes.

Jim Buckley. Saks Fifth Avenue, Beverly Hills, mid-1950s. This display is really about passion, not clothing. As the show card says, quoting Shakespeare, "He took the bride about the neck / And kissed her with such a clamorous smack / That at the parting, all the church did echo."

78 | Designer unknown. B. Altman, New York, 1952. A shoe window of calculated disarray with a frankly commercial attitude that in no way detracts from its humorous satire. The woman who couldn't make up her mind was a common theme of display windows.

Warren McCurtain. Gunther
Jaeckel, 1955. "My budget was
low," McCurtain remembers.
"'How much can a roll of
cellophane cost?' I asked
myself."

Gene Moore. Bonwit Teller, New York, 1955. Caught in the web of a delicious spoof, the public believed that the model in this photograph, taken by Moore, was a woman: In fact it was a man. The designer was besieged with calls from modeling agencies wanting to know who the woman was. "Sorry, but she's returned to Sweden," was his reply.

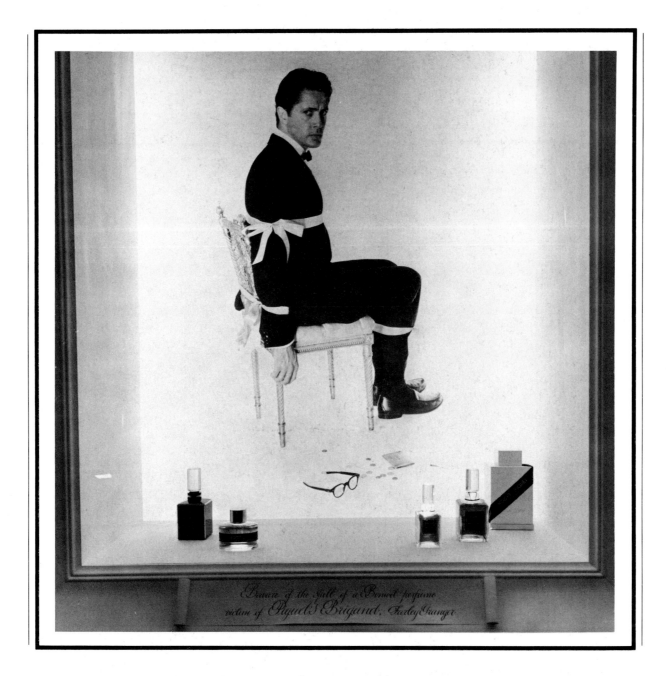

Gene Moore. Bonwit Teller, New York, 1950. Moore photographed Farley Granger as a "victim" for this "Beware of the Spell" fragrance promotion. The concept was inspired by Alfred Hitchcock's *Rope*, then playing, in which Granger had starred.

Jim Buckley. Saks Fifth Avenue, Detroit, mid-1950s. "Toiletries."

82

Jim Buckley. Saks Fifth Avenue, Beverly Hills, mid-1950s. "*Tout ou rien!*"

83

84 | Henry Callahan. Lord & Taylor, New York, 1953. A child's Christmas dream of an angelic orchestra playing the music of the spheres, which was piped out to the street.

Henry Callahan. Saks Fifth Avenue, New York, 1957. It took a year of preparation to achieve this Easter vignette, complete with specially commissioned rubber babies and motorized cradles.

85

Henry Callahan. Lord & Taylor, New York, 1950. Iconoclastic for its time—the fifties were a period of conventional display—this window featured a likeness of Michelangelo's *David*, eternal symbol of male beauty, to announce an exhibit of men's fashions since the 1400s.

ADAM IN THE
LOOKING GLASS

A resume of men's fashion
since the 14th century.
A preview of men's clothing
of the future as proposed
by prominent women designers.

Now at the Costume Institute
of the Metropolitan Museum
of Art

Tommy Rowland. Dayton's, Minneapolis, 1961. This Christmas window was inspired by *The Wind in the Willows*. Rowland says of it, "My biggest problem was how to make a rat presentable."

Jack Quinn (*left*); John Kearn and Jack Quinn (*above*). Bergdorf Goodman, New York, early 1960s. Shadowbox windows, often reduced still further by masking, are ideal for featuring jewelry. The one on the right is a real, water-filled aquarium.

89

Louis XV

90 | Tommy Rowland, Len Shimota, and Joseph Wright. Dayton's, Minneapolis, 1963. "Marie Antoinette." Real roses framed this three-dimensional re-creation of a Fragonard painting. A true example of the impermanence of display art, this window could last only a few days.

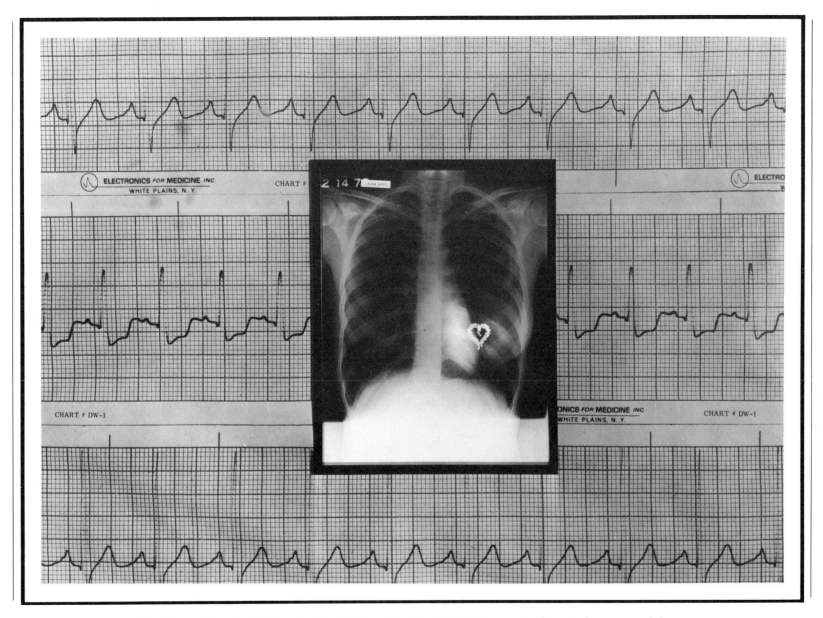

Ray Mastrobuoni with Ron Smith. Cartier, New York, 1972. To create this window, a model was X-rayed wearing a diamond brooch. The X-ray was mounted on a Lucite board and shown against an EKG chart that had been found in a hospital trash bin. The display caused a stir among the city's physicians, some of whom called in to report that the person whose chart was used was in serious danger of an attack. Mastrobuoni displayed the real brooch in an adjoining window, accompanied by surgery equipment in vermeil.

91

92 | Gene McCabe. Cartier, New York, late 1960s. Pearls spill from one of the shiny oyster tins.

Gene McCabe. Cartier, New York, late 1960s. McCabe placed cellophane in front of moving lights to create an aurora borealis as background for a crowd of candles and one diamond solitaire.

93

Gordon Ryan. Bloomingdale's, New York, 1974. Rope wedgies perched on a huge rope wedge.

94

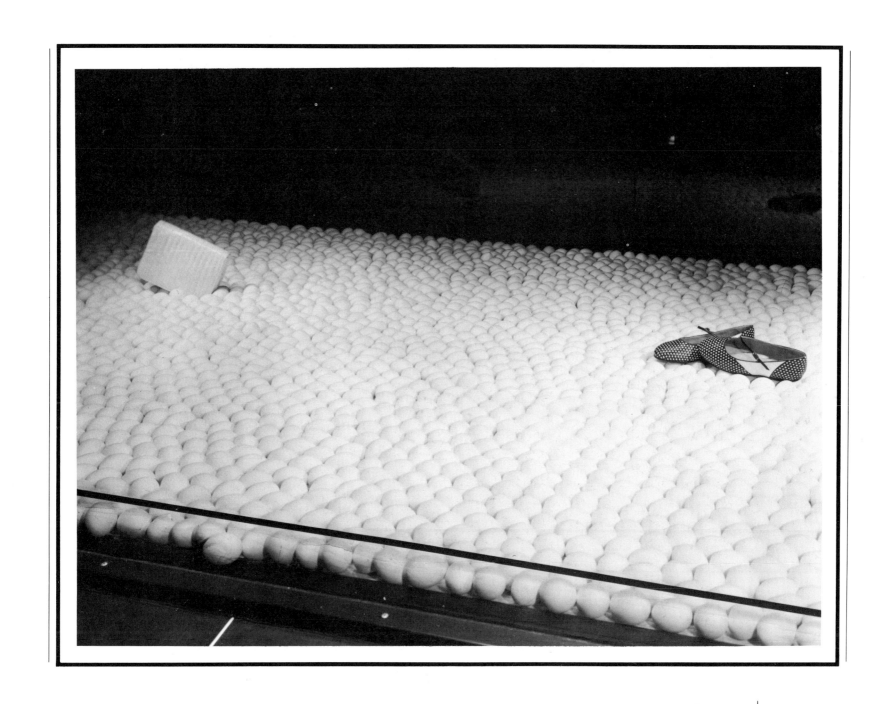

Reggie Smyth. Charles Jourdan, New York, late 1970s. The window floor was covered with over a hundred dozen fresh eggs.

96 | Dan Jones. D. H. Holmes Co., New Orleans, late 1970s. Wooden Lilliputians tie up their wooden Gulliver—with ties.

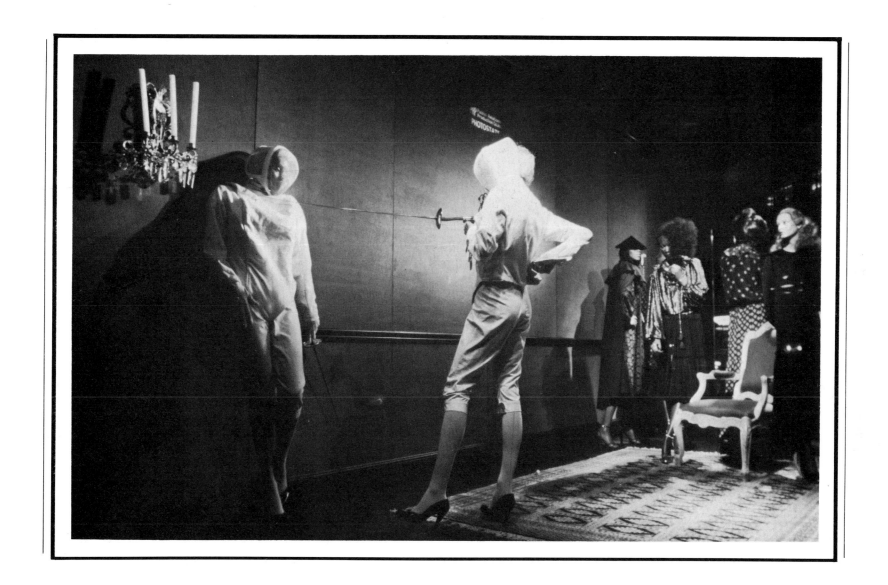

Candy Pratts. Bloomingdale's, New York, 1978. | 97

Gene Moore, with assistant Ron Smith. Tiffany, New York, mid-1970s. A silver string holder displayed against a background of skillfully tangled plumber's string, chosen by Moore for its flexibility and fuzzy softness.

98

Gene Moore, with assistant Ron Smith. Tiffany, New York, 1978. A work of art done to sell enameled eggs.

Robert Benzio and Richard Currier. Saks Fifth Avenue, New York, 1978. A game played with scale and age.

Robert Rufino. Henri Bendel, New York, 1977.

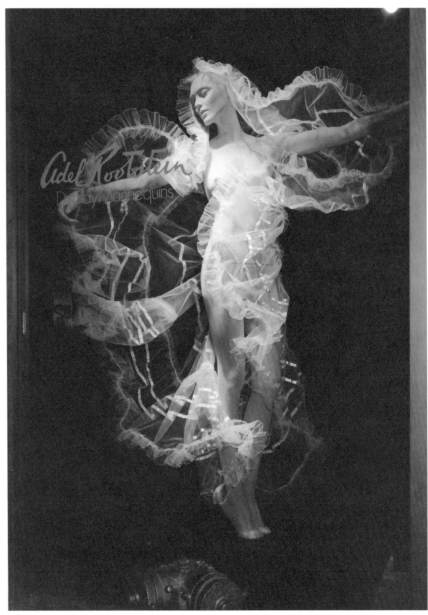

102 | Michael Southgate. Adel Rootstein, New York, 1977. The merchandise was the mannequins themselves.

Reggie Smyth. Charles Jourdan, New York, 1978.

Mike Stephens. Z.C.M.I., Salt Lake City, 1977.

105

Guy Scarangello. Barney's, New York, late 1970s. Scarangello is one of the few window artists allowed the freedom to do interesting work with men's wear. While male mannequins have often been used to enhance women's windows—as escorts or accessories—they have rarely been in the spotlight. This has been due in part to the less flexible nature of men's clothing—one can't do that much with a suit—and in part because store management has usually had a rigidly traditional view of how men's clothing should be shown.

107

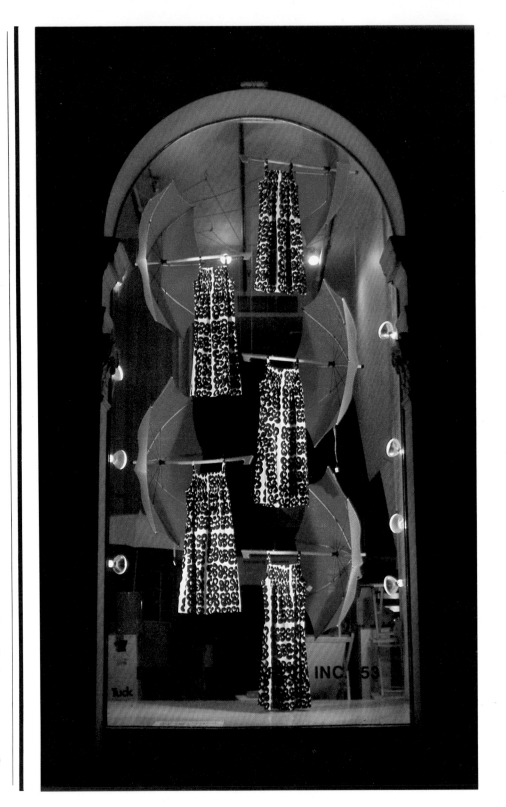

James Schultz. Design
Research, New York, 1977.
Parasols shaded sundresses in
a huge three-story window.

108

INTERLUDES
HANAE MORI
PLAZA COLLECTIONS
FOURTH FLOOR

Sonny Jaen. Bergdorf Goodman, New York, 1977. Jaen found the arms abandoned in the basement and recycled them. Tight budgets are often the mothers of improvisation.

John Boiano (*above*); Richard Hillman (*below*). Macy's, New York, 1977. Hedgehogs and mannequins: tulle to the teeth.

110

Candy Pratts. Bloomingdale's, New York, 1978. White porcelain emerged from a mound of black coal, like an archeological treasure recently excavated.

Frank Myers. Carson Pirie Scott, Chicago, late 1970s. An insomniac sheep counting men.

Howard Meadows. Bloomingdale's, New York, 1980.

114 | Frank Myers. Carson Pirie Scott, Chicago, late 1970s.

Frank Myers. Carson Pirie Scott, Chicago, 1973. Amusing juxtaposition of mustaches and bow ties.

116 | Sheridan Kane. Gimbel's, New York, 1979.

Henry Callahan. Saks Fifth Avenue, New York, 1970. This mirrored mannequin was designed by Mary Brosnan, premier mannequin maker. Callahan wrote on the back of the photo: "Breathtaking! and crowd stopping *de luxe*."

Bob Baron (*left*); Ray Mastrobuoni (*right*). Cartier, New York, 1979. The turkey wore a dinner ring. Garlic was an ingredient in the window (*right*), installed as part of a Fifth Avenue tribute to Italy. Unfortunately, it had to be removed after just a few days—under the hot lights the garlic began to deteriorate, unleashing a pungent scent into the store.

Celeste Cecchini. Z.C.M.I., Salt Lake City, 1978. Wired silk and a wind-swept porcelain figurine.

Richard Currier. Saks Fifth Avenue, New York, 1978. An example of what window artists call "bringing the garment to the ultimate." This *coupe de théâtre* manages to create the illusion of space in a shallow (4' 9" deep) window.

Howard Meadows. Bloomingdale's, New York, 1980.

122 | Larry Laslo. Bergdorf Goodman, New York, 1979. "The Writing's on the Wall." For this graffiti window, Laslo recruited three teenagers off the street and had them spray-paint the dress designer's name, Richard Assatly, all over the wall.

Candy Pratts. Bloomingdale's, New York, 1978. The designer in a playful mood.

Stephen de Pietri. Henri Bendel, New York, 1981.

124

Stephen de Pietri. Henri Bendel, New York, 1981.

Scott Morehouse. Z.C.M.I., Salt
Lake City, 1979.

126

Robert Mahoney. Gump's, San Francisco, 1979. Gold insects gathering around the flame.

127

Tom Lee. Bonwit Teller, New York, 1941. Lee was one of the first display artists to tell a story in his windows. The dapper thief represented the jeweler Schlumberger; the conceit was that he was taking his own creations to use in fabric design.

128

# TOM LEE

"I ALWAYS EXPECTED PEOPLE TO COPY ANY-thing good," Tom Lee once said. An important display artist, one of the first to make a name for himself, he had seen his own work copied virtually everywhere. But it did not upset him. Unconventional and imaginative as he was, he always had another idea to explore.

Lee was born in Costa Rica, the son of a member of the American Consular Service. He spent his early childhood in Brazil, whose bright colors and festive spirit influenced his later designs. By the time he reached his teens, Lee's interest in the arts had been firmly established, and he left home to go to the Traphagen School of Design, and later to the National Academy of Fine Arts. During his school years he would stay awake night after night, perfecting his skill at drawing. Sculpture, however, turned out to be his favorite medium. He spent his spare time doing freelance work, designing costumes for

Minskey's, posters for MGM, book jackets for Modern Library, and paper sculptures to be used in photographs for *Harper's Bazaar*.

At the age of nineteen, Lee went to work at Macy's in New York, laying out advertisements, sketching fashions, and designing individual shops within the store. A while later, he took a trip to Australia as a design consultant and apparently liked the country, for he spent several years there. By the time he came home he had established himself as a Surrealist painter.

Lee returned to New York in the early thirties, and was appointed display director at Bonwit Teller. The job gave him a chance to try out his Surrealist techniques in three-dimensional spaces. He was also able to employ other talented artists, allowing them to use his windows as *fenêtriers*. Salvador Dali collaborated with him for a time, until a disapproving management tried to tamper with one of his designs. Furious, Dali ejected his fur-lined bathtub through the window and out onto the street. Dali's outburst and subsequent arrest became a cause célèbre in window lore.

Lee's approach to windows was essentially pragmatic. He followed the premise that the themes developed for window displays should be based entirely on the merchandise being shown. This method, and his practice of working closely with buyers and others in the store hierarchy, most often enabled Lee to reconcile the contrary demands of merchandising and art. He believed that windows were intended to deliver a message and that the best way to do this was to emphasize the obvious over the subtle, display over design. The time element was essential. There was no time to "take in" a window gradually, as one could an interior; so his windows were designed to catch the eye instantly. Being a perfectionist, he often wrote his own copy for the window show cards. And he knew fashion inside and out.

Bonwit Teller was a large store, so Lee often found himself designing windows at the last moment. Under this pressure, he developed a talent for improvisation. Once, exasperated with an expensive but limp wig that he had placed on a mannequin's head, he picked up another just like it and hammered it on top of the first to give them body. A co-worker of his once said in admiration, "He could close the windows down to an inch."

While working at Bonwit Teller, Lee also found time to design costumes and sets for Lincoln Kirstein's American Ballet and for several Broadway shows. In one year, his creative hand was involved in five musicals, one of which was *Louisiana Purchase*. He created movie promotions, fashion shows, and sets for the World's Fair. His designs and displays charmed thousands—"By 1941," one colleague said, "New York was his."

When World War II broke out, Lee joined the war effort, employing his special talents as chief Air Force camoufleur in London. He

131

developed many new methods of camouflage, which were taught at his Academy of Camouflage. One of his inventions was a pulley and string system that could cover an airplane in two minutes. Another was a floating set of tiny, twinkling lights, ingeniously set up to imitate the outline of London and draw off bombers.

He also helped out with morale-boosting. One of his telegrams to the home front asked, "Please send four pounds sequins." The confused recipients thought it was a code; but Lee was in earnest—he needed the sequins for a troop play called "Skirts."

At the Normandy Landing, Lee witnessed some looting and, sensitive to the artistry involved, described G.I. tanks that "lumbered up front with mannequins in rude positions, riding aloft with parasols and curtains draped on them. Bedsteads, chickens, pillows, or flowers covered the vehicles. . . ." When they arrived in Paris, Lee discovered that the Germans had been well aware of the psychological effect of windows. "Lots of the shops looked as if there'd been no war. Those windows really looked luxurious, until we learned that the Germans had forced the French to dress their windows even if the shop was empty . . . to convey a false sense of normalcy."

After the war, Lee returned to New York, where he began to design lobbies, ballrooms, restaurants, and offices. It was perhaps here that he found his forte: a field in which he could combine a sense of interior space with the dramatic flair of display. One of his great successes was the RCA showroom in Radio City Music Hall. He also designed small packages for the cosmetics of Elizabeth Arden, Helena Rubinstein, Lily Daché, and Coco Chanel.

In 1947, Tom Lee Ltd. was formed, a firm that did design and consultant work. Its first major client was Bergdorf Goodman, for which Lee was in charge, as he said, "of just about everything—windows, interiors, and fashion shows." He later specialized in hotel interiors, traveling around the globe on various projects. During the fifties and sixties, he became involved in designing Fifth Avenue parades, charity balls, and museum shows for the Metropolitan Museum of Art, the Philadelphia Museum, and the Smithsonian. He created commercial products, including the Dove soap bar. Faced with the design of a Christmas display for Rockefeller Center, he decided to tie it in with the design of Saks Fifth Avenue across the street. The result was a graceful procession of angels lining the mall.

Tom Lee died in 1971, of injuries sustained in an automobile accident. He had believed that beauty is not in the eye of the beholder, not subject to personal interpretation—beauty exists in and of itself; sensitive, aware people are able to see it and create it. Lee left behind scores of beautiful creations, from gracious lobbies to delicate perfume bottles—and of course he left his windows, perhaps more precious because they now exist only in the memories of those who saw them.

134 | Dana O'Clare. Lord & Taylor, New York, 1940. This window managed to evoke nostalgia while carefully avoiding the insipid sentimentality to which many Christmas windows fell victim. The "frost" sprayed on the window was a combination of epsom salts and stale beer.

# DANA O'CLARE

IT IS A CLEAR WINTER NIGHT IN DECEMBER 1937. From the windows of Lord & Taylor, the low, muffled sound of bells resonates along Fifth Avenue. In the store's long bank of windows huge golden bells made of papier-mâché swing from side to side as crowds of people press close to get a better look and to drink in the magic of the season that the windows celebrate. The bells are display artist Dana O'Clare's Christmas present to the city of New York and a window display unprecedented in the annals of retailing: the first recorded noncommercial use of store windows in the city. O'Clare, a sprightly Irishman with an irrepressible streak of humor, had won the heart of New York at the age of twenty-four.

O'Clare confesses that his love affair with the world of the stage and costume design started at an early age. He attended the Beaux Arts School in Montreal, and at the age of twenty-one moved to New York to take a job at Gimbels. O'Clare wryly recalls that, at the time, the store was making an effort to rid its staff of "truckdrivers"—people who were just doing their jobs, but were not especially creative or involved with the store.

Most of the mannequins in those days were wax and imported from Europe. True to Continental style, they were anatomically correct. Male models, remembers O'Clare, were labeled "small," "medium," and "American," according to the size of the genitalia. One of O'Clare's first jobs was to file the nipples off the female mannequins, thus rendering them fit for use in a respectable store window.

Before long, O'Clare moved on to Bliss Display, one of the first companies to produce props exclusively for display purposes. O'Clare asserts, however, that his window career did not begin in earnest until the summer he went on loan to Lord & Taylor. Dorothy Shaver, a champion of the non-traditional who was vice president at the time, immediately recognized his innovative creativity and arranged quickly and permanently to steal him from Bliss.

It is impossible to discuss O'Clare's career without reference to Shaver, the merchandising genius who was convinced that the fine arts were vital to her business and that they even contributed to sales. She understood, says O'Clare, the exact needs of display artists and made every effort to nurture them and protect them from the tyranny of rigid minds. Her credo was "If it makes people talk, let's do it!" She espoused the concept of "publicity" rather than "advertising." To her, the image of the store was paramount; selling and merchandising always came second. As she once said, "We evolved the basic concept that we should publicize rather than advertise; that we should sell the store first and the merchandise second; that we should push ideas rather than items." According to O'Clare, this philosophy established Lord & Taylor as the leader in the field of display art for many years.

In nine short months under Shaver's tutelage, O'Clare rose to the position of display director. He viewed himself as a stage designer. He learned to rely on his own ingenuity rather than upon elaborate props, feeling that although props might be lovely, they were too often unrelated to the merchandise. He also learned to manipulate lighting as an artist would a paintbrush, washing the backgrounds of his windows with exotic color. When his patience ran out with the many limitations of the huge, heat-generating light bulbs of his day, O'Clare approached a Yale theater designer and a lighting man from Century Lighting and asked them to design a thousand-watt bulb that would fit into a Fresnl box, creating a sort of small-scale spotlight. They did, and it allowed him to make the most of the natural foil of nighttime, a dramatic effect hitherto denied display artists.

With his famous Christmas windows, O'Clare had pioneered the use of recorded sound in windows. He was also the first display artist to introduce olfactory display by diluting the perfume featured in a window and pumping it out to the sidewalks by means of a DeVilbiss atomizer. And by using curved recessions that formed a striking contrast with the straight walls framing his window canvas, O'Clare created the optical illusion of greater depth.

O'Clare took great delight in experimenting with the "staginess" of Surrealism that swept through New York in the thirties. The aim of his windows, he says, was "to awaken a memory, a wish, a desire, dream, or need," and he measured the success of his windows by the amount of pleasure they gave the public. He did not hesitate to use shock value from time to time—whether humorous, educational, earthy, or just plain commercial—to avoid the bland predictability he described as "beating on the black keys too long." Many of his windows illustrated future events—balls, openings, society parties—keeping a step ahead of the window-gazers. One April Fool's Day, for example, O'Clare placed contorted mirrors in the windows—just for the day—a daring idea that attracted thousands of people to peer at themselves in the glass.

As display director, O'Clare maintained a policy of protecting the staff from what he felt were irrelevant store regulations prohibiting outside work. It was a good way of ensuring the loyalty and morale of his team. Says O'Clare, "The store had a policy that no one was allowed to do the windows of any other stores. On my walks around town, I would occasionally spot one of the boys doing display on his day off, jobs the store obviously didn't know about. Well, the salary they were getting was low, so I just decided to keep my mouth shut."

For the most part, Dorothy Shaver fought off the buyers and stylists who objected to O'Clare's work by curtly asking, "Who is display director around here anyway? Besides, I've seen it and I like it!" Once, however, she was powerless to ward off criticism. This was the day that Walter Hoving, then president, called O'Clare and asked him to remove a window that consisted of a red lacquer table upon which mice were skating, scratching figure eights in the veneer. O'Clare was furious and flew up to Shaver, who was having her hair done in the beauty parlor. She admitted that she loved the window, but pointed out that Hoving *was* the boss. Hoving, in the meantime, had attended a meeting of the board where he was greeted by enthusiastic praise for the very window he had complained about. Hoving dashed to the phone and instructed O'Clare to disregard his orders, but it was too late—the disputed display had been removed. "It was a bad day for Mr. Hoving," O'Clare recalls with a smile.

In 1941, O'Clare left Lord & Taylor to join the war effort. The Office of War Information quickly took advantage of his talents by having him arrange publicity shows all over Western Europe. These exhibits, entitled "Since 1939," were usually staged in the local city hall and were meant to fill the news gap created by the chaos of war.

O'Clare came back to America four years later and jumped into a new career—creating display materials and doing design consultation for the private showrooms of J. P. Stevens and Cannon Mills. His eyes gleam when he remembers these post-war years: "The power I had, the power to do what I wanted to do, without any interference—it was exhilarating."

Throughout the years that were to follow, O'Clare never lost his fondness for window art, and today he is just as feisty about the politics of display as he was when he was in the thick of it. He is opposed to the current trend toward hiring outside display consultants rather than calling on the talents of a staff. It is, he feels, not only demoralizing to the store's artists, but overpriced. He still maintains that "the best display man is only as good as the management behind him"—management that should have the good sense to give its display artists the freedom and authority they need to carry out their ideas. "You hired the display man as an expert in style, color, and design," says O'Clare, speaking to an imaginary executive. "So trust him to know his business. Don't try to impose your own taste on the windows. If you cannot stand the current styles or colors, grin and bear it."

What are the ingredients that make up the ideal display person? O'Clare answers with characteristic humor: "He must have the curiosity of a cat and the tenacity of a bulldog, the friendliness of a child and the patience of a self-sacrificing spouse, the diplomacy of a wayward mate, the enthusiasm of a movie fan, the assurance of a Harvard grad, the humor of a comedian, and the tiresome energy of a bill collector."

And, perhaps, the courage of a dreamer—to imagine a window without merchandise, just bells pealing down Fifth Avenue, sending a message of peace among men.

Henry Callahan. Saks Fifth Avenue, New York, 1958. The high society club El Morocco, with its zebra banquettes, was re-created in a vision of the socialite life, one of Callahan's favorite themes.

142

# HENRY CALLAHAN

HENRY CALLAHAN BEGAN HIS DISPLAY career at a tender age, in the hot-house environment of Waldron Academy. This exclusive Philadelphia school, steeped in a curious mixture of Victorian fantasy and class-conscious Main Line propriety, had a strong effect on the young boy. Callahan remembers the hushed atmosphere of the chapel, where an almost pagan splendor contradicted the stilted decorum of school officials. His early scholastic life revolved around the excitement of various theatricals, feast days, and holidays when he decorated rooms and draped the cold stone walls and statues of the school in colorful materials. He recalls that he was particularly fascinated by the dramatic ceremony involved in the professing of nuns. For him, it was a fashion show—the vestal brides of Christ, solemn and resplendent in satin wedding gowns, moving down the aisles, their snowy trains gliding over the crimson carpet, to take their vows.

By his early twenties, after a year spent as a display artist at Bonwit Teller in Philadelphia, Callahan had established himself as display director of Lousol's, a small Philadelphia store. But by 1936 he was dissatisfied—making it big meant New York's Fifth Avenue, and Callahan came to realize that he could not settle for less. Taking a cut in salary, he engineered a position as fashion coordinator at Lord & Taylor in New York.

The New York that greeted him in the mid-thirties was a throbbing city, just recovering from the Depression years and caught up in the full swing of the Deco movement. Manhattan's social upper echelons were ruled by a sleek and sophisticated crowd—a group who welcomed those involved in fashion or on its periphery, and who opened their arms to artists of distinction. Callahan's childhood fantasies—escorting debutantes, dressing in white tie and tails—were finally fulfilled. Society was extravagant. The Duke and Duchess of Windsor ruled fashion; hats and gloves were de rigueur; proper people dressed for dinner. Callahan exploited the dress codes, rites, and migration patterns of the various birds of high society as they moved from Newport to New York to Palm Beach. Their mode of life thematically influenced his windows: hunt breakfasts, junior cotillions, polo matches, El Morocco, Broadway openings, and the opera were his subjects. His renderings of these events were influenced by Cecil Beaton, whose work Callahan admired.

When Dana O'Clare left Lord & Taylor for the European war theater, Callahan, kept off the battlefield by a heart murmur, replaced him as display director. During Callahan's tenure, Lord & Taylor became one of the principal trend-setting establishments in Manhattan. Each day, long lines of limousines formed in front of the store, which made a point of catering to the needs, the gilded life-styles, of the upper classes. Lord & Taylor's big budgets allowed for grand, expensive, "bang-up" windows. What Boldini or Helleu did for the Marchesa Casati and Princess Greuftheule, Callahan was able to do for the leading society figures of his day. He had the talented mannequin maker Mary Brosnan cast the likenesses of such women as the Duchess of Windsor, Babe Paley, and Gloria Vanderbilt into mannequins for his windows. Fervent fans of window display would gather out front one night a week to watch the unveiling of the new displays.

Lord & Taylor was still under the tandem direction of Hoving and Shaver. With their support, Callahan's expansive concepts were promoted and sold to the board of directors, thus ensuring liberty for his staff to create the special tone and aura Callahan desired for the store. Shaver adopted Callahan as a protégé the way she had O'Clare, protecting and applauding his handiwork. Shaver controlled all sales and promotion efforts, skillfully creating an image for the media. She was aided by the remarkable illustrationist Dorothy Hood, whose fashion sketches did so much to stamp the store's image of quality and chic in the minds of the public. One man who worked with Shaver, Callahan, Hood, and Hoving described them as a productive "team that rowed in the same boat, heading for the same shore." Shaver later became president, and the image remained on course, navigated through war and peace by Callahan, who remained with the store until 1952.

Callahan was assisted by two superbly talented men, Paul Voegler and Dick Eastwood. Voegler, with an uncanny ability to take new display materials and use them in unexpected ways, created the marvelously elaborate stage effects favored by Callahan. Eastwood was a fashion aficionado whose ability to accessorize the mannequins was without peer. With staple gun and paint, feathers, satin, silk, and miles of tulle, they helped Callahan magically re-create rich scenes of elegance from the patrician life. In the Lord & Taylor windows, passers-by could glimpse swank, self-assured, moneyed people moving about in a chinoiseried, ormolued world of antiques, *objets d'art*, priceless carpets, and pink candles in silver sconces. It could be said that Henry Callahan gained entrée into society by displaying it.

In 1952, Callahan moved to Schenley's, and then in 1954 he went to Saks Fifth Avenue. At the time, Saks was a decided contrast to the reserved femininity of Lord & Taylor. Its atmosphere was masculine, and its image was that of a dressy store, somewhat extreme, with many specialty shops. In one weekend Callahan swept through the store and changed the Saks image from one of glitter and sequins to conservative class. His bold move was a great success, and he remained at Saks for the next twenty years, shaping and guarding its elegant image until 1974, when he reached mandatory retirement age. He now works as a consultant, dividing his professional time between Revillon in Paris and the Philadelphia Museum of Art. Callahan has returned to his native city, an established and revered member of the sophisticated society he once viewed from afar.

148 | Robert Benzio. Saks Fifth Avenue, New York, 1978. A party thrown by Yves Saint Laurent aboard a Chinese junk to launch his new perfume, Opium, was the inspiration for this display, in which sleek clothing is set off by spiky, fantastical flowers.

# ROBERT BENZIO

**R**OBERT BENZIO OF SAKS FIFTH AVENUE laid the foundations of his career in window display while still a child. "I was," he says, "a strange boy, drawing and dressing dolls." He had a lonely, nonconformist childhood—a pattern many display artists describe. He grew up isolated, unhappy about society's disapproval of him. But he has overcome that pain by allowing it to be the source of the creation of beauty. And so this "strange" child has turned into a showman par excellence: His windows at Saks are full-blown theatrical fantasies with all the chic panache of a Baron de Meyer. Benzio's thirty-one windows in the main store in New York aim at perfection. His imprimatur assures meticulous execution and almost fanatical attention to detail, habits that he learned during his apprenticeship with Anton Heller at B. Altman & Co.

According to Benzio, the best display ideas are direct and uncomplicated; his windows are stunning in their streamlined, self-assured simplicity and daring. They are elaborate without being over-done, coordinated without being boringly safe. To three basic colors already used he will add one more—the special and adventurous last step that lifts a Benzio composition out of the ordinary.

Benzio's checkered, pyramid-like career has caused others to cluck disapprovingly. Within a decade, he moved—with unabashed ambition—from B. Altman to De Pinna to Best and Co., back to B. Altman, and then on to Bergdorf Goodman. Benzio admits that all this time he had in mind one goal, the position he has held since 1976: vice president and head of display for Saks. "It was the only position in New York I wanted," he says.

It was obvious that Saks wanted him, too. Over the years, the store has given him the budget and freedom he required. "They met my needs, and it's good to know I no longer have to beg," says Benzio candidly.

He has gone to the highest bidder, and what he has given in return is a luxurious image to the already sophisticated store shaped by his predecessor, Henry Callahan. One of Benzio's first moves was to remove all but one of the traditional carved wooden ribbons that had proclaimed the store's name for thirty years. ("If you don't know this is Saks," he says, "you're really in trouble.") He completely changes the backgrounds of the comparatively shallow windows five times a year, a task that would be prohibitive to a store with a smaller budget. Thirty-two handpicked people work with him in the main store, along with an additional four regional directors and thirty-one display managers from branch stores. His influence is evident across the country.

Today, Benzio does not put in the windows himself. He directs his staff, teaching them his art, guiding their creativity. And he edits the work, often adding that final Benzio touch.

Benzio's current joy is to open new stores. Working closely with the architects, he is asked what *he* wants. He can specify window dimensions, cover his prosceniums so that they disappear, dictate which type of lighting, carpeting, and fixtures to use—in fact, he can design all the elements that go into creating the Saks environment.

What does Robert Benzio see in his future? Ideally, he would like to tackle the biggest window display of them all—the theater. Until that time, "the Avenue" will continue to be his audience, and the price of admission is free.

152 | Candy Pratts. Bloomingdale's, New York, 1978. A keen-eyed observer would notice that the shattered prisms do not match those that have remain unbroken.

# CANDY PRATTS

**C**ANDY PRATTS IS A ROSE FROM SPANISH Harlem, a determined young woman whose talent and energy took her on an astounding trip to fame and fortune at Lexington Avenue and Fifty-ninth Street—Bloomingdale's. Long before her career took off, Pratts had decided that the old cliché of the poor, starving artist was not what she had in mind. After completing a two-year stint in merchandising at New York's Fashion Institute of Technology ("I found I hated buying"), she took a job as an assistant photographer and stylist at Bachrach's ("lots of airbrush"). Her next job, in the early seventies, was selling shoes at Charles Jourdan ("I wasn't wearing $100 shoes then—$80 shoes, yes, but not $100 shoes"). There was no opening in window display: Jourdan's had imported a woman display artist from France, not trusting the freer American approach. Pratts waited patiently. Soon the woman went back to France, and she got her chance. Viewing Jourdan's windows as an empty canvas, she boldly offered her services for a conditional three-month period, stating that she would voluntarily vacate the position if they were not satisfied.

With no budget, but equipped with a brash imagination that more than compensated for the monetary limitations, she moved in. Shoe straps that had been allowed to hang limp were starched upright for a crisper look. Unthinkable objects—an ancient toilet, shattered champagne glasses—took their place on august Fifth Avenue. Pratts commissioned artists to do windows, giving them an open gallery on one of New York's busiest corners, and forwarding the careers of several, including illustrator Michaele Vollbracht.

Her success drew the attention of Marvin Traub, president of Bloomingdale's, who offered her a position as head of display at his store. Pratts was justifiably nervous that corporate limitations might be imposed on her. Knowing that she would fail if she felt stifled, she bluntly told Traub that if she accepted the job, she would do "no toning down." Traub replied that it was precisely her brand of nonconformity they were looking for.

Pratts accepted the challenge. At twenty-four she had one of the most important jobs of her profession. What followed was display history. But first she had to adjust to several major conditions. For one thing, she was no longer limited to shoes—an entire range of merchandise from gowns to gadgets was hers to fool around with. For another, she was no longer allowed to do any of the windows herself: Bloomingdale's is unionized, and only union members are permitted to work in the window space. She would have to direct through the glass from the sidewalk.

Pratts took all this in stride and immediately began to make radical changes. She combined two separate windows on the prime corner to form one large triangular space—a play area that soon became her favorite window. Of course, having this much space did not necessarily mean she would use it all; to Pratts, a lone mannequin made just as much dramatic impact as a herd.

Determined to make her mannequins expressive, she defiantly taped, rebolted, and screwed them into postures and positions they were never expected to assume. Many fellow display people thought she had discovered new, more flexible mannequins, not realizing that Pratts's own ingenuity was responsible.

As opposed to most display directors, she decided not to pick out the merchandise intended for her windows. Says Pratts, "I didn't want them coming to me and saying, 'Well, you picked it and it didn't sell.'"

Then she took the boldest step of all: She reintroduced the "situation window" to the seventies. There were many who did not appreciate the raw and often shocking subject matter of these windows, but Pratts claims, "I wanted to make this field valid again, to cause people to become aware of the people involved." She drew more publicity to her controversial psychodramas than displays had garnered since the post-war years, when they were reported weekly in columns and hundreds of people strolled along Fifth Avenue to "do" the windows. Once again, the media were paying attention to what display directors were up to. Local and national television, newspapers, and magazines began avidly to report on the latest occurrences behind the glass.

All this pleased Pratts, who firmly believes that the raison d'être of display is not to sell but to entertain and to attract. "If windows can do this, then when the store closes, the windows will go on selling," she says. She also believes that these "attractions" ought to project the aura of the store. "After all, you can buy a Klein, Lauren, or Saint Laurent dress in half a dozen stores around town. What brings the customer to a particular store is the image the window sells. The customers should be able to see themselves in whatever theme the windows set up." For the affluent young class that flocks to the trendy mecca they fondly called "Bloomies," Pratts's displays mirrored the life they either led or would have liked to lead, and they entered the store in pursuit of that illusion.

For four and a half years, Bloomingdale's was Candy Pratts's exclusive fiefdom: She managed an empire of 105 people, forty windows, eight floors. Five full-time carpenters churned out the props for her productions and four electricians ensured the proper atmosphere for her pyrotechnics. She once said her approach to the job was "I've got to get off on it or I quit." And enjoy it she did, even though the extremely public nature of her work made her feel deeply vulnerable to criticism. After all, she freely admits, it was her ego up there big as the window, and she had to fight constantly to protect both it and her integrity. "You can fire Miss Pratts, but you can't take out her window" is the way she summed up her attitude toward censorship. Eventually, her influence extended across the country to fourteen branch stores. Several times annually she would wing around the world, examining firsthand the markets and bazaars that supplied her store with its merchandise. Dealing with an executive board meeting soon became as familiar to her as wielding a staple gun.

In 1979, Pratts left Bloomingdale's, figuring it was time to do something else, to try to succeed independently. She is now a freelance consultant to the retail trade in fashion and catalogue design, and is preparing to be an art director in films.

What would she do if asked to work on windows as part of a store plan? She envisions audio-tech windows with outside speakers that would play environmental tapes—crackling leaves for fall fashions, the sounds of birds, breaking glass, mannequin conversation—living windows that would bring back Pop Art. In response to charges that she slid back into more conventional and accepted display modes toward the end of her window career, she scoffs, "I didn't tone myself down. The public merely adjusted. Any social change will appear first in the arts. Artists are simply the ones who are daring enough to state something."

Candy Pratts's daring, assertiveness, humor, and taste for rebellion have made her a pioneer in a field virtually dominated by men. In her window career, she generated a series of psychodramas that upset, entertained, inspired, and—in the end—mocked a world that takes itself entirely too seriously.

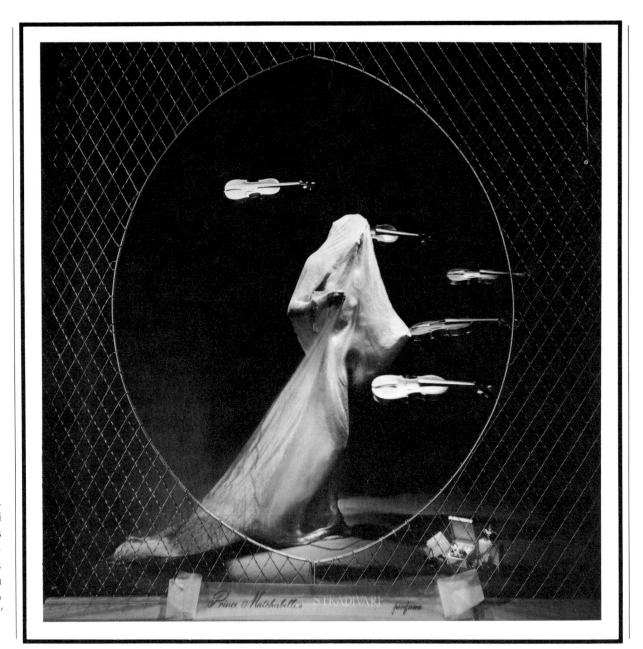

Gene Moore. Bonwit Teller, New York, 1945. "Stradavari Perfumes." Moore remembers that "the mannequin was gold-leafed and nude, and fans blew the rose-colored China silk so that it was tight up against her body."

# GENE MOORE

"I'M ONLY A WINDOW TRIMMER," SAYS GENE Moore, a glint of humor playing in his otherwise sad gray-blue eyes—a window trimmer with the choicest corner in America as his stage: Tiffany. Gene Moore has spent a lifetime struggling to maintain his identity, resisting the pervasive climate of mediocrity, and triumphantly presenting his dreams as displays—the expressions of a man who has contemplated life rather than taken it for granted. He tends to share the often lonely perspective of other display artists. But now he is their most renowned representative and an acknowledged genuis of the world of window art.

Part of Moore's talent rests in his ability to see rare qualities in commonplace dime-store objects and to juxtapose them with a maharajah's ransom of gold and jewels. Surprise is the primary ingredient in these concoctions, and heresy the impetus. Gleefully discarding the dark velvet pads so telling of the dreary history of jewelry display, Moore boldly scattered the exquisite Tiffany treasures on earth and pebbles, teasingly dropped them onto trowels, and playfully set them on ropes, strings, nuts, and bolts. The resulting tiny miracles astonished and delighted the public, and incidentally revived the art of displaying jewelry.

Moore started as a painter, but quickly decided that "if I couldn't be the best painter in the world, I would be the best window trimmer." He apprenticed himself to Jim Buckley at I. Miller in 1936. In 1939, he moved to Delman, the shoe emporium at Bergdorf Goodman, where his work first received serious attention. At Bergdorf he had the chance to collaborate with Robert Riley, who was in the display department there until the end of World War II.

Moore's big break came in 1945 when he was offered the position of display director at Bonwit Teller. Once he was there, his work followed its own intriguing and unpredictable path. His Easter windows blossomed with real planted flowers, quickly becoming a traditional part of New York's yearly welcome to spring. His exceptional shoe displays incorporated a mirror below the window so potential customers could observe the unfortunate condition of their own shoes while viewing the pristine merchandise spread before them. His love of the theater took form in amusing and dramatic vignettes long before the controversial "situation windows" of the seventies were done. He also put in serious windows: "Most people don't want to think," he claimed. "Windows that make you think are important." Eventually, he began lending his services to the neighboring store, Tiffany & Co., and, for a time, he managed to do them both.

In 1961, he announced to Bonwit Teller that he was leaving to take a permanent job at Tiffany. The president, in an effort to make him stay, asked him to name anything he wanted. "To begin with," said Moore, "I want the main floor to be devoted entirely to display. I want there to be no limitations as to window size. The windows should be totally flexible as well as refrigerated and heated [to allow for the use of perishables]. And I want to be able to use fire, air, and water in my displays."

"But, Gene," the president protested, "you know that's impossible!"

"Exactly," replied Moore. "That's why I'm leaving."

With his move to Tiffany, Moore found his ultimate direction as an artist. Walter Hoving, Tiffany's president, the former employer of O'Clare and Callahan, is guided by the credo "A window should never try to sell merchandise." To Moore, he said, "I want you to make the windows beautiful according to your own taste. Don't try to sell anything. We'll take care of that."

To this day, Hoving firmly believes that if a store is going to employ an artist, it must give him freedom. According to Moore, "This

163

freedom is one of the greatest things in my life. As an artist, one must experiment. If you don't, you may as well slit your throat." And he, in turn, has extended this freedom to others. He hired unused talents—Robert Rauschenberg, Jasper Johns, James Rosenquist, and Andy Warhol—to design the backdrops for his windows. Of course, he himself placed the jewelry in the often unusual settings.

Moore's talent is as multi-faceted as the Kohinoor: He is a portrait and fashion photographer and a designer of jewelry, costumes, and stage sets. But when it comes to surveying the peaks and valleys of his work, he is critical: "The majority of what has been done in display should disappear off the face of the earth and I'll put half of mine with it." Recently, he has developed a yen to return to jewelry design. He says wistfully, "To them, I've arrived. To me, I haven't. It hasn't happened. I haven't really done *the* thing. But I'll probably keep on going until they find me toes up in a window box."

In the meantime, behind the several layers of alarm-protected glass and plastic, he continues daily to mesmerize the audience of thousands that pursues his bejeweled fantasies. It is evident that the people and the muses are still with him.

# BIBLIOGRAPHY
# PHOTO CREDITS

# BIBLIOGRAPHY

For background on window history and the nature of the art:

Buckley, Jim. *The Drama of Display*. Pellegrini and Cudahy, New York, 1953.
Gaba, Lester. *The Art of Window Display*. Studio Publications, New York, 1952.
Leydenfrost, Robert J. *Window Display*. Architectural Book Publishing Co., 1950.
Marcus, Leonard S. *American Store Windows*. Whitney Library of Design, Watson-Guptill, New York, 1978.

# PHOTO CREDITS

by C. F. Weber Photography, courtesy of D. H. Holmes Co.; *page 116:* photograph courtesy of Gimbel's; *page 98:* photograph by Nick Malan Studio, courtesy of Tiffany & Co., Gene Moore, Display Director; *page 99:* photograph courtesy of Tiffany & Co., Gene Moore, Display Director; *page 101:* photograph by C. P. Smith, courtesy of Henri Bendel; *page 102:* photographs by Sandy L. Studios, courtesy of Adel Rootstein; *pages 104, 105, 119, 126:* photographs courtesy of Z. C. M. I.; *pages 106, 107:* photographs by Ralf Manstein, courtesy of Barney's; *page 110:* photographs by Fifth Avenue Display Photographers, courtesy of Macy's; *pages 97, 111, 113, 121, 123, 152:* photographs by Willo Font, courtesy of Bloomingdale's; *pages 112, 114, 115:* photographs courtesy of Carson, Pirie, Scott; *page 118:* photographs courtesy of Cartier; *pages 120, 148:* photographs by Fifth Avenue Display Photographers, courtesy of Saks Fifth Avenue; *page 122:* photograph courtesy of Bergdorf Goodman; *pages 124, 125:* photographs courtesy of Henri Bendel; *page 127:* photograph courtesy of Gump's; *page 152:* photograph courtesy of Bloomingdale's; *back jacket:* photograph by Sandy L. Studios, courtesy of Adel Rootstein

pd